MODE DRAWING

**INSTRUCTED
BY ISAO YAJIMA**

ATORIE
KO

CONTENTS

INTRODUCTION

The drawing of fashion illustrations is at its most wonderful when they are done according to each individual's sensitivity. This book focuses on the achievement of such expression and is aimed at those people who aspire to become fashion designers. Using actual garments as reference, it explains the various points, right from the rough sketch stage to completion, and goes over the treatment of garment line and detailed designs, as well as how to give expression to the material and the use of color.

In this book, clothing design is dealt with in two distinct structural groups. The first of these is the most simplistic clothing form, which is called the prototype, and is the basic form, or, in terms of fashion, line, which excludes any exaggerated aspects of design or ornateness in the fabric used and any other decorative aspects. The second group incorporates the decorative aspects—that is, all kind of aspects relating to frivolous and fun features, such as exaggerated expressions and the particular surface characteristics (texture, etc.) of the fabric. Due to such important factors as the sense of period and function, and also creative inventiveness, the blending of these two structural groups gives way to a myriad of design variations.

In the midst of today's vast variety in garment types and the diverse ornamentation available, it is becoming increasingly important to work with the prototype as the basic garment form, in order to draw designs or illustrations that communicate the charming characteristics of the particular garment.

When looking at garments that exclude decorative aspects, the basic form (prototype) of these garments can be readily determined. For example, the line of a sporty jacket and a classic tuxedo are of different structures, and if they are compared to clothes which have the structure of shirts, the prototype will be completely different again. In short, each aspect of the garment's structure is built from the relationship of refined functional beauty. Balance is achieved in this way, which is why it is called the prototype. Breaking the shape of the garment in darkness or just sketching big, loose designs is not a very desirable habit to fall into.

Garments are not just drawn straight on top of bare skin. There are obvious spaces between the garment and the body which conceal a number of functions. In addition to providing volume on the design side for the garment's line, this space is also a functional space which eases the contact between the body and the fabric. Topics dealt with, include how to present this space in designs, how to sketch the space existing between the body and the fabric so that it shows movement, and how to portray the garments in an attractive pose in sketches. Therefore, it is necessary to have eyes that can judge the degree of separattion or looseness between the body and the fabric, and where exactly this occurs by just looking at the outer form.

今日のファッションは，その歴史がそのまま語れるような20年代〜60年代のあらゆるスタイルが見られます。東洋美あり西洋美あり，クラシックあり，モダンがある。ミニもあれば，ロングもある。ボディフィットありオフボディがある。—というように，スタイル，丈，シルエット，そしてテイストに至るまで，実に多様化しています。更に，それらをコーディネイトすることにより，また新たなスタイルやテイストが生まれます。そんな中で，〝作る〟〝描く〟という立場からデザイン画をより明解に，また魅力的に描くためにドローイングはもちろんのこと，モチーフとなるラインの典型的な形，基形像（プロトタイプ）と人体との関係をよく理解することが大切です。

このプロトタイプとは時代の創造的な造形感覚や伝統美，合理的構造理論によって組みたてられるもっとも簡素化した服の形です。つまり，素材，色，装飾的技巧などデザインとしての付帯的要素の一切を省いた姿のことです。

このプロトタイプを輪郭線で捉えた陰形をシルエット，又は服のラインと呼びます。

デザイン画表現の初めの練習ではプロトタイプの分量がどのように体と係っているかをよく観察し，ヌードプロポーションの上から描いていきます。そこでは身体にフィットし体の線を感じさせる部分，体から離れ，服としてのムーヴメントをつくるルーズな部分とをラインの特徴として生かし，人体のリズミカルな動きと合わせ，活き活きとした服の表現をすることが大切です。また，既に完成している服をイラストレーションにして描く場合も同様で，その服のプロトタイプを捉えポーズとシルエットとの関係を素描します。

幾つかの服種を組み合わせた着こなしの場合もプロトタイプを一着ずつヌードプロポーションに重ねて描いていきます。

又，人体を服の大きさに合わせディフォルメすることは禁物です。本書はスケッチから着色までの工程を，画材の巾をしぼり，まずデザイン表現の第一歩として人体と服とが描けるようになることを目的に解説しています。

デザイン画はあくまで2次元（平面）としての発想や，証明，伝達手段であり，実在する形や状況とは多くを異にします。従って表現されるモチーフは具体性のみ要求される訳ではありません。描き手は自由に題材から自分の発想する世界を描き，画に置き換えるのです。

TIGHT-FIT LINE
タイトフィットライン

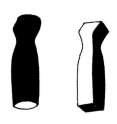

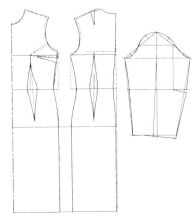

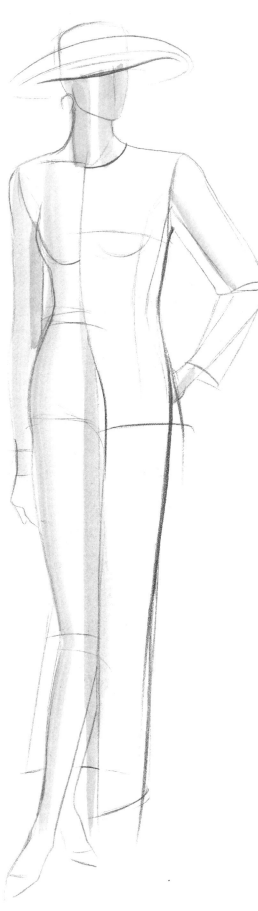

TIGHT-FIT LINE is an overall body-hugging line, with minimum looseness.
The line of the body, just as it is, is turned into clothing. In the design, the unique image of the worn apparels body line and clothing comes to life by drawing the body precisely.

最小限のゆるみをもち，ボディ全体にそったライン。

体の線がそのまま服になったといった形です。

デザイン画では体を正確に描くことでボディラインと服との独特な着装イメージが生まれてきます。

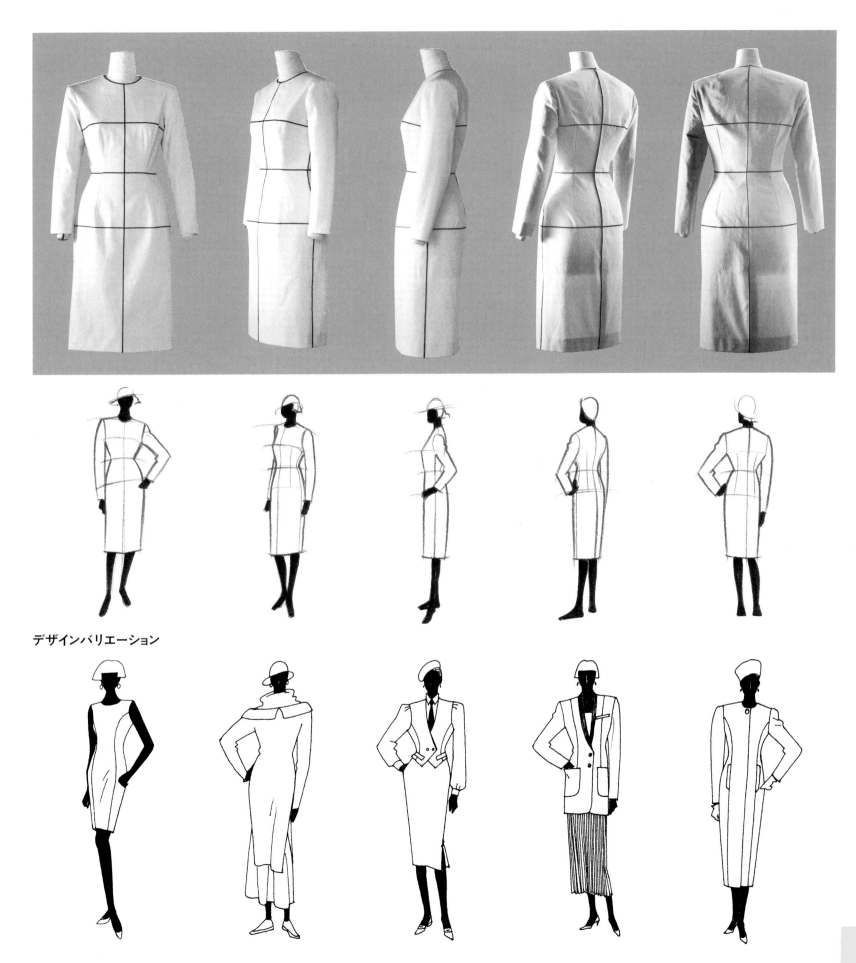

デザインバリエーション

FIT & FLARE LINE
フィット&フレアーライン

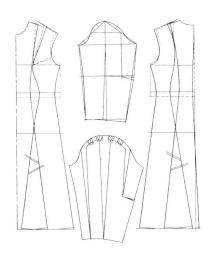

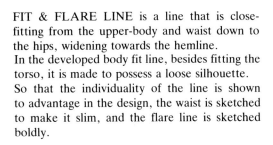

FIT & FLARE LINE is a line that is close-fitting from the upper-body and waist down to the hips, widening towards the hemline.
In the developed body fit line, besides fitting the torso, it is made to possess a loose silhouette.
So that the individuality of the line is shown to advantage in the design, the waist is sketched to make it slim, and the flare line is sketched boldly.

上半身，ウエストからヒップにかけてフィットし，裾にむかい拡がったライン。

ボディフィットラインの発展した形で，トルソー（胴体）部分にフィットポイントを持ち他はゆるみを持たせたシルエットになっています。

デザイン画では人体のウエストをスリムにディフォルメさせ，拡がる裾を大胆に描くことでラインの個性が生きてきます。

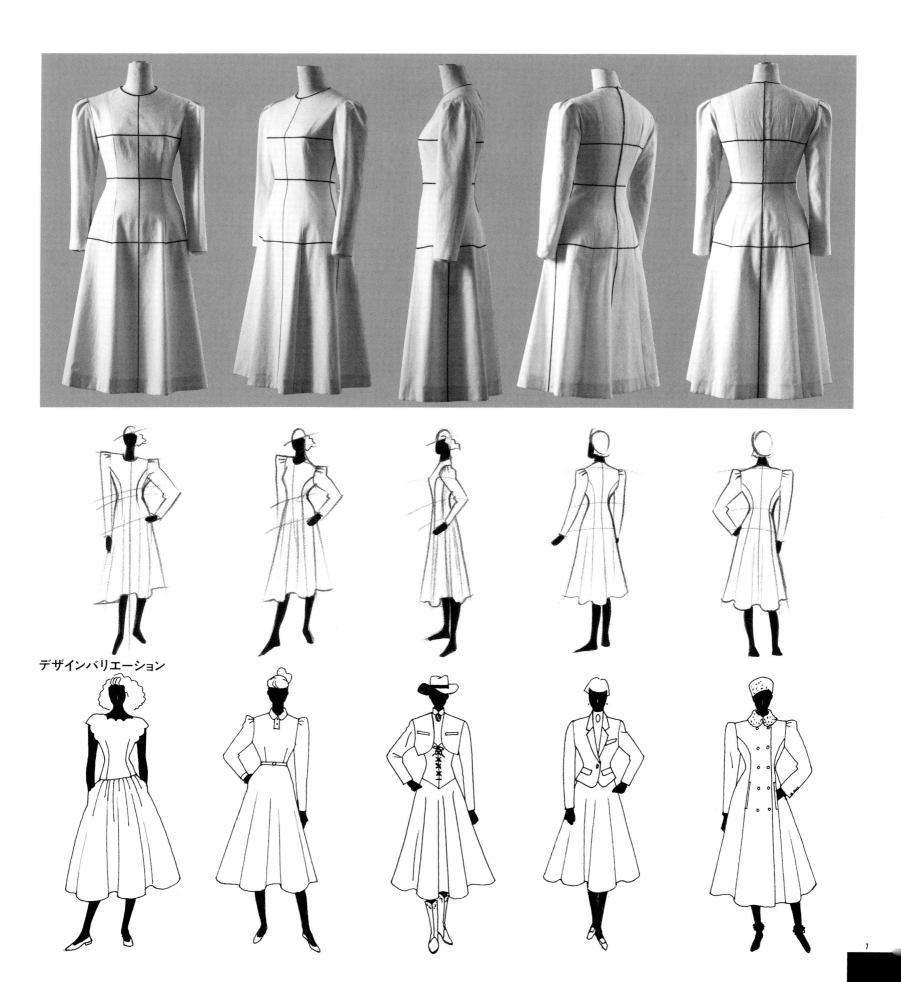

デザインバリエーション

RECTANGULAR LINE
レクタンギュラー（ストレート）ライン

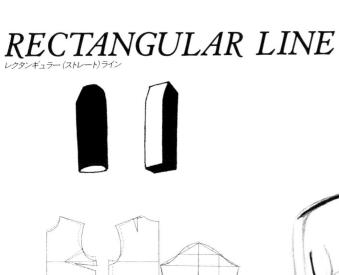

RECTANGULAR LINE also known as the straight line, this line is a rectangular box-shaped line, with uniform looseness, neither hugging too close nor flaring disproportionally away from the body line.

The line which the off body line is based on, consists of drawing the silhouette rectangular from all sides—front, back, left, and right.

別名ストレートラインは，ボディ全体につかず離れずの均等なゆるみを持った直方体のライン。オフボディラインの基になるラインで，シルエットは前後，左右の四面からなる直方体として描きます。

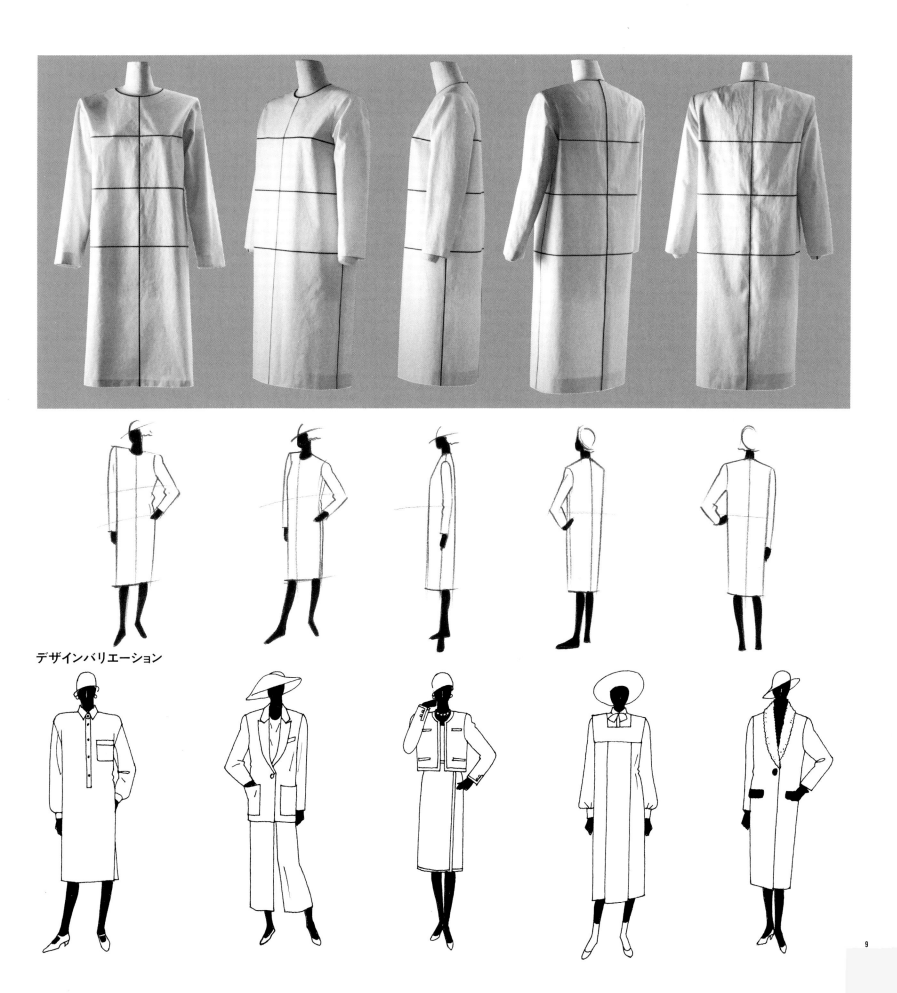

デザインバリエーション

INVERTED TRAPEZE LINE
インバーテッドトラペーズ（逆台形）ライン

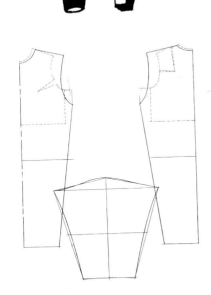

INVERTED TRAPEZE LINE is a line evoca-
tive of a V-shape, with its widest point at shoulder breadth, tapering narrowly towards the
hemline.

In one variation of this line, the shoulder width
and the breast width are increased, and the Y
line of the long torso is made to appear long as
far as the waist line. With this line, the top half
of the body has the shape of an inverted
trapezoid. A feature of this line is that depending on the shoulder pads and the off shoulders,
the width of the shoulders and the looseness of
the armhole is exaggerated. When you draw this
kind of silhouette it is important to draw the
body appropriately, and as a point in the design,
allow what room you can between the clothing
and the body.

肩巾を広くとり，裾に向って細くなっていくV
型を感じさせるライン。

このラインのバリエーションの1つには肩巾，
胸巾にボリュームを持たせ，ウエストライン ま
でを長く見せるロングトルソー（長い胴体）の
Yラインがあります。このラインの上半身は逆
台形を持ち，肩パッドやオフショルダー（袖付
けを外に持つ）によって肩の広さや袖ぐりのゆ
るみが誇張されているのが特徴です。こうした
シルエットを描くときは，人体を適切に描き，
服と人体との間に出来る空間をデザインのポイ
ントとして描くことが大切です。

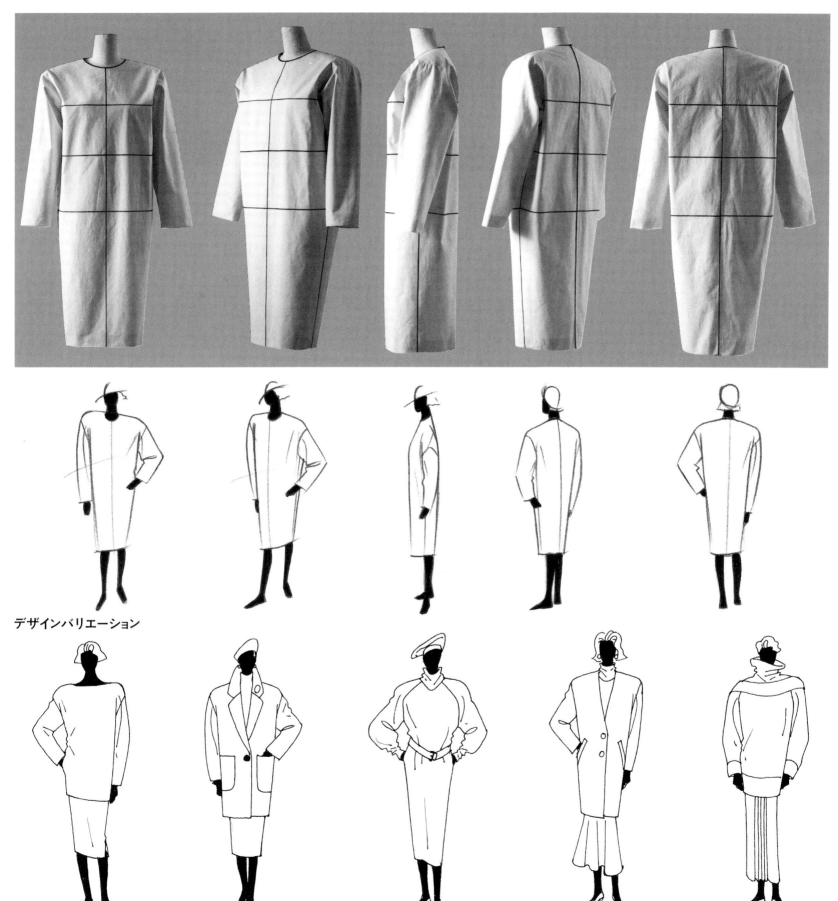

デザインバリエーション

OFF-BODY LINE
オフ・ボディライン

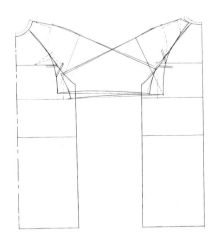

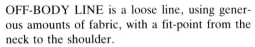

OFF-BODY LINE is a loose line, using generous amounts of fabric, with a fit-point from the neck to the shoulder.

It is a point in drawing, that with the line of the clothing being seperated from the body per se, the size of the whole piece of clothing should be loose, and the proportions of the body should be slim.

ネックから肩にかけフィットし，布をたっぷり
とったルーズなライン。

文字通り体から離れた服のラインで，服全体の
大きさはゆったり，人体の分量はスリムに描く
ことがポイントです。

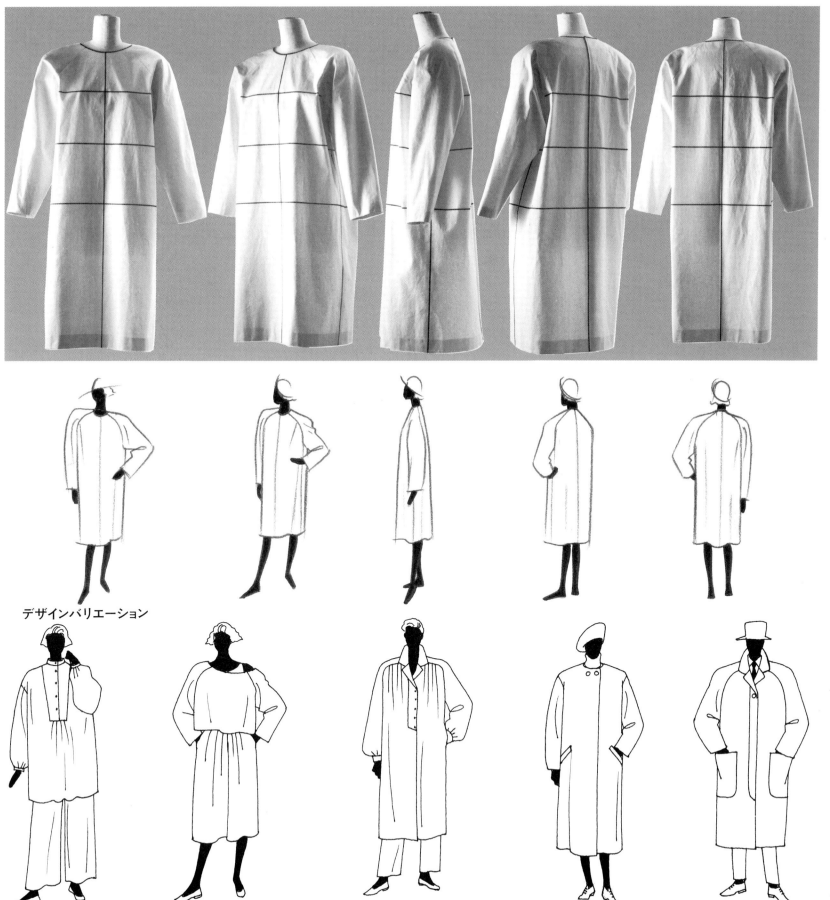

デザインバリエーション

TENT LINE
テントライン

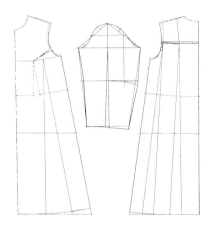

TENT LINE is a line, whose fit point is from the shoulder to the arm line (i.e. chest line), while widening towards the hemline.

The ample spacing between the body and the clothing becomes flared drapes towards the cuff, but while the breast, the neckline, and the shoulder line are slightly exaggerated, they still fit. Bulky tent lines are either deep, shallow, abundant, slight, etc., with the shape of each drape different depending on the material. Ascertaining the type of material before sketching is very important.

ショルダーからアームラインにフィットポイントを持たせ、裾にむかって拡がったライン。

ボディと服との間にある、たっぷりとしたゆるみは裾に向かい更に拡がったドレープとなりますが、胸の上、ネックライン、肩線は、多少誇張しつつフィットしています。分量の多いテントラインは深い、浅い、多い、少ないなど、素材によりドレープの形がそれぞれ異なってきます。素材を確かめて描くようにすることが大切です。

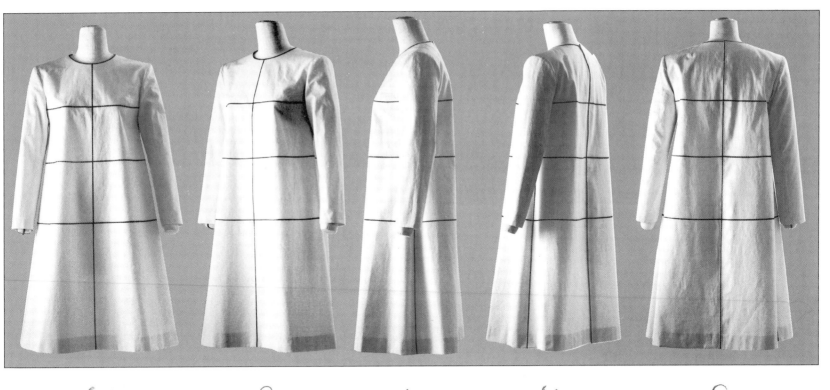

デザインバリエーション

BLOUSON LINE
ブルゾンライン

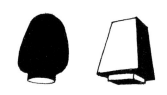

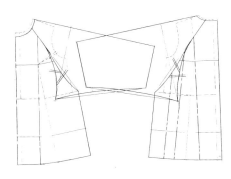

BLOUSON LINE is a blousey, billowy line, with a generously full-volumed hemline.

The silhouette is expressed in a round shape, but depending on where the folds of the material, and the gather, are stablized, the roundish effect will change. The resultant appearance of the blouson comes to life if the body is drawn slim.

たっぷりとした分量の裾を適度に絞ったライン。シルエットを丸形で表現しますが，布の張り具合，又，ギャザーを体のどこで安定させるかによって，丸みをつくる効果が変ってきます。人体を細身に描くことでブルゾンの表現効果は生きてきます。

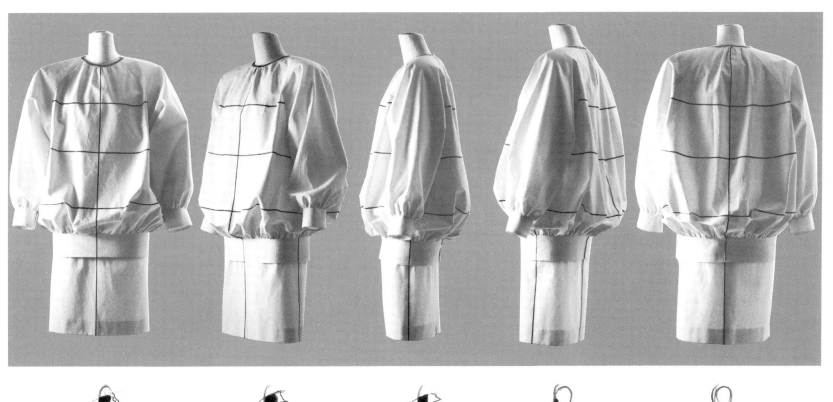

デザインバリエーション

DRAPE (FOLDS)
ドレープ

D rape (folds) is one of the essential elements with regard to the expression of costumes. In this book, the elements involved in creating drape are dealt with in two district categories.

One is hanging drape, which takes on virtually the same form as the folds of a curtain as it hangs down from a curtain rail. The second is drape, which is created by pulling. For example, in the case when a curtain is lifted up and caught back, curved folds are created in the fabric. That is, they are created by a gentile pulling between the top of the drop and the caught back portion of the fabric. Further, depending on the degree of the pull's force, the depth of drape (folds) created in this situation will vary.

In regard to its relationship to costumes, drape can be divided into two further elements. One is those drapes, whose shape is created in the design itself; and those that are created in conjunction with the body's movements. Using the characteristics of these kind of drapes effectively in designs, serves to give animation to the movement of the garment, while at the same time, bringing to life the reality of the body and the costume.

ドレープ（ひだ）はコスチューム表現にとって欠かせない要素の一つです。このドレープの出来る要因を本書では大きく二つに分けて捉えています。
その一つは垂れるドレープで，丁度カーテンレールから下がったカーテンのひだのような形態です。二つ目は引っ張られて出来るドレープです。例えば下がったカーテンをなにかでひっかけて持ち上げると，布にたわみが生じます。つまり，下がった基とひっかけ部分とで軽く引っ張っている状態になります。又それは引き具合の強弱によってドレープ（ひだ）の深さ浅さも変わってきます。コスチュームとの関係においてドレープを更に二つの要因に分けることができます。その一つは，デザインとして形づけ（テーラードされている）られて出来ているもの，着たときに体の動きに係わって出来るものとがあります。このようなドレープの特徴がデザインの中で生かされることは，服の動きを活き活きとさせ，併せて人体とコスチュームのリアリティーも生きてきます。

TRIANGULAR

TRIANGULAR is a triangular-shaped drape, which is created from the drop, when the fabric is pinned up in two places.

トライアングル

2ヶ所を支点にして，吊り下げられたときにできる三角形のドレープです。

CYLINDER

CYLINDER is a cylindrical or tubular drape, which hangs in a straight drop from a pinning in one section.

シリンダー

1ヶ所を支点にして，真っ直ぐに垂れる筒状のドレープです。

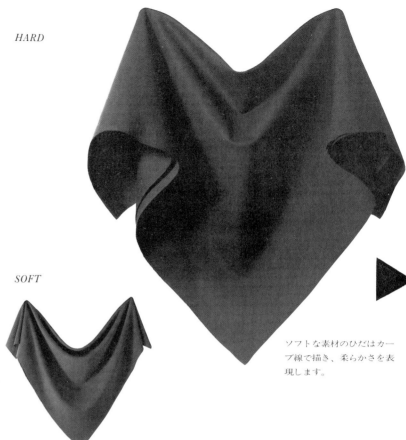

HARD

SOFT

ソフトな素材のひだはカーブ線で描き，柔らかさを表現します。

ハードな素材のひだは布の張りの調子を直線的なタッチで描きます。

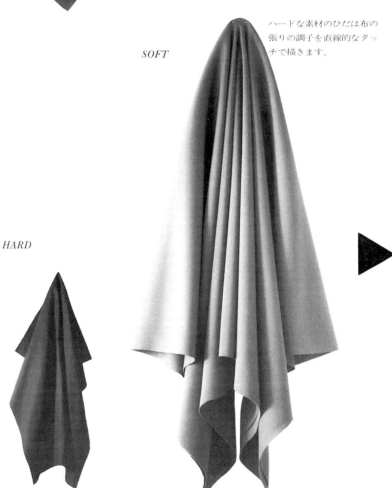

SOFT

HARD

HARD

SOFT

19

GATHER

GATHER is a zigzag-shaped drape, whose drop is created when multiple sections are pinned up.

ギャザー

複数の支点を寄せて垂らしたときにできるジグザグ形のドレープです。

HARD

HARD   *SOFT*   *HARD*

SPIRAL

SPIRAL is a drape, which—when tubular fabric is pulled from left and right, the tubes bend into loops—looks like circles turning.

スパイラル

筒状の布を左右から押すと輪のように筒が屈折し，丁度円が回転しているようにみえるドレープです。

SOFT

HARD

HARD

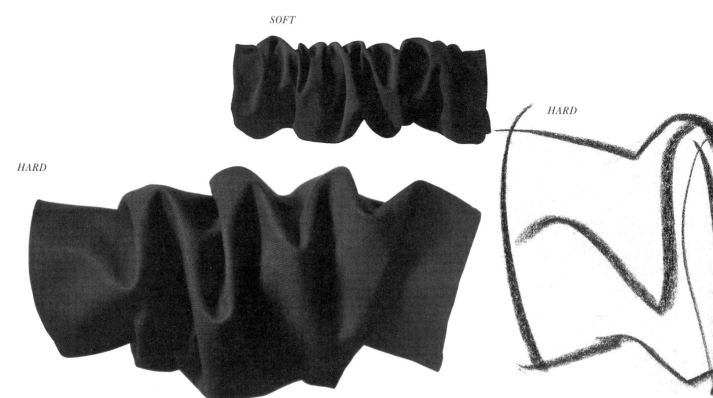

SOFT

HARD

SOFT

HARD

WAVE

HARD

SOFT

WAVE is an undulating, hill-shaped drape, which is created when evenly placed fabric is pushed from left and right, or from top and bottom.

ウェーブ

平らに置いた布を左右、又は上下から押したときにできる丘陵のような形のドレープです。

HOOK

SOFT

HARD

HOOK is an intersectional (crossing) shaped drape, which is created when evenly placed fabric is pushed from left, right, top and bottom, or from a multiple of directions.

フック

平らに置いた布を左右、上下、又は複数の方向から押してできる交差形のドレープです。

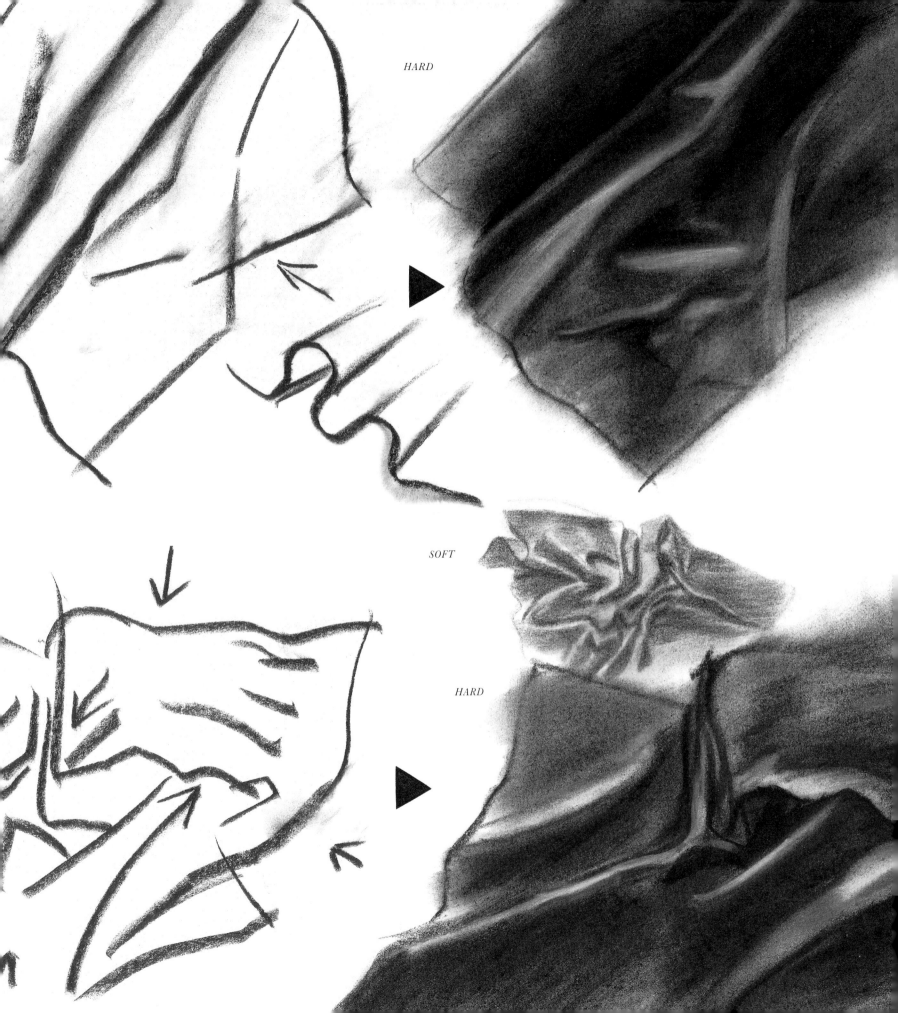

HARD

SOFT

HARD

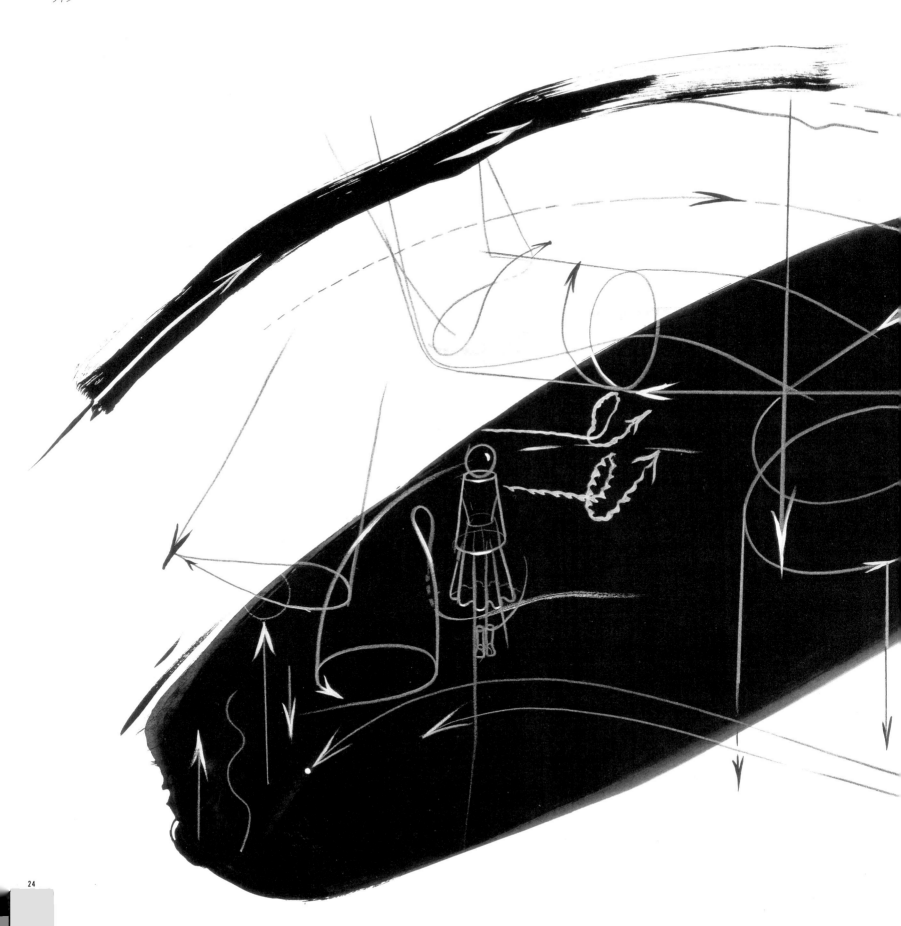

With regard to lines, there are straight lines and there are curves. Of straight lines, these are perpendicular lines, horizontal lines and oblique lines. Straight lines, which run in the direction from top to bottom, express falling (fall), while those in the opposite direction, express rising (rise) or partitioning (division). Oblique lines are for depth, while horizontal lines express width and breadth. In a picture, by expressing the form and also the direction of movement, these lines proceed to depict space.

In drawing design pictures, it is essential, that the various aspects that exist—or are capable occurring—between the body and the garment, and also the extent of volume involved, is captured by these lines.

For example, if in a picture, one were to draw a gentle curve perpendicularly, the left and right arcs on the outside and inside of the curve's bounds will begin to take on the semblance of a portion of a garment. And by swinging the line around further, movement (dynamic motion) is given to the volume, and it is possible to draw the states ranging from the stationary to the moving.

線には直線と曲線があり、直線の中には、垂直線、水平線、斜線があります。上から下に進む直線は落下を、その逆は上昇をあらわし、また分割をあらわします。斜線は奥行きであり、水平線は幅をあらわします。それらが画面の中に、形態や運動方向を描き出します。

デザイン画を描くには、人体と服との間に存在する、また起こりうる様々な面と体積の状態を線で捉えることが必要です。

例えば、両面にゆるい曲線を一本たてにひいてみると、その曲線を境に、左右の弧の内側と外側が服の一部であるように見えてきます。そして、更に線を回転させることにより、そこには体積のムーブメント（躍動）が生まれ、静から動を描くことができるのです。

MATERIAL
マテリアル

・地塗りの濃度

薄塗り

a

中厚塗り

b

厚塗り

c

aterials are dealt with by classification into 6 elements.
1. Degree of thickness (Transparency)
2. Degree of stiffness
3. Degree of coarseness (Density)
4. Degree of brilliance (Luster)
5. Degree of nap raising
6. Degree of heaviness
These degrees are expressed by using the strength of the line and controlled by the density of the primary coating.

素材を６つの要素で区分して捉えます。

１．薄い厚いの度合い　　（透明度）

２．硬い軟らかいの度合い

３．粗い細かいの度合い　（密度）

４．光沢の度合い

５．起毛状況の度合い

６．その他、重い軽いの度合い

これらの度合いを地塗りの濃度によって調節し、
線の強弱を使って表現します。

透明水彩では重なった色調が
生かされます。

不透明水彩では下地色は消え、
後から重ねた色になります。

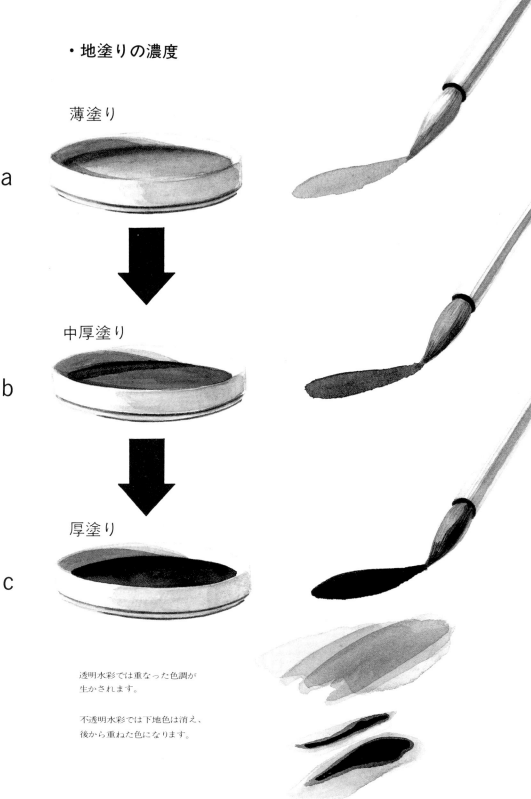

1．水で薄く溶いたポスターカ
　ラー絵具で下塗り
2．クレヨン（OIL PASTEL）
　を叩くように塗る
3．濃い目のポスターカラー絵
　具を塗る

In a picture, things of large mass show materials that are thick, stiff and fine in density, whereas conversely, things of small mass show materials that are thin, light and coarse in density. The expression of a material is drawn by using the degree of density of the paint layers and the strength of the lines, in consistency with the mass. To show differences between materials, the differences are expressed by means of the contrast to the feel of the adjoining materials. For materials which are closely similar and whose differences are hard to distinguish, the differences are emphasized.

Order of drawing is: 1) the primary coating; 2) drawing, in order, the touches of the surface variations to express the feel of the fabric.

Further, a number of tools and methods can be employed such as: scratching or making indents on the paper; scraping off parts of the already painted surfaces before the paint dries; using water repel action; rubbing with one's finger; using an erasing pencil or tissues; placing paper on a rough, uneven surface and rubbing over it; using collage techniques; and using netting and so forth. By using a number of these various techniques in conjunction with one another, we will proceed to give expression to the different materials.

絵の中で質量の大きいものは、厚い、硬い、密度の細かい素材を表し、逆に質量の小さいものは、薄い、軽い、密度が粗いといった素材を表します。質量の表現は塗りの濃さの度合いや、線の強弱を使って描きます。描く順序は①下塗り②表面の変化のタッチ順に描き入れ、布の素材感を表現します。

又、紙をスクラッチ（引っかいてキズをつける）したり、一度描いたものを乾かないうちに削ったり、水のハジキを利用したり、指でこすったり、擦筆やティッシュペーパーを使ったり、デコボコの材質の上に紙をあててこすったり、コラージュ（切り貼り）したり、網ブラシを使ったりなど、道具のいろいろなもの、様々なテクニックをかけ合わせて、各々の素材の表現をしていきます。

white

カットワーク
クレープ
ファンシークレープ
金巾
ローン
羽二重
ギンガム
クレープデシ
アートピケ
サッカー
ハニーコーン
デニム
ドンゴロス
パイル
コードレーン

1．ストライプの巾に合った平
　筆を使い、薄く溶いたポス
　ターカラー絵具を下塗り
2．ストライプを交差させる
3．交差した四角な面に、濃い
　目の絵具を塗る

1．水で薄く溶いたポスターカ
　ラー絵具を下塗り
2．織りの線を入れる
3．パイルの丸みのタッチを入
　れる

リボンヤーンレース

オーガンジー

ボイル

Light

キルティング

オストリッチ

チュールレース

1. で薄く溶いたポスターカ
ラー絵具を下塗り
2. 筆に白色をつけ、紙で水気
をとり、筆先がバラバラに
なったら、筆のタッチを利
用して描く

フロッキー

ファー

1. パステルエンピツで凹凸部
分の線を描く
2. 指で線の方向に沿ってこす
る

チュールレース

1

2

シャンタン

箔

白い部分、明るい灰色部分、暗い部
分の三段階のモアレ模様を描くには

型押しベルベット

モアレ

1. 白い部分は残して（紙の白
い地を生かすよ、明るい灰
色で下塗り
2. 暗い灰色部分を塗る

キャンバス

別珍

コブラン織り

リネンクロス

1

2

33

Depending on the characteristics of the type of fiber used (long, short, coarse, fine), the strength of the ply, the thread arrangement and the coarseness of the intertwinement and so on, various different types of style and mood can be created. Moreover, depending on the final finishing treatment (e.g. nap raising and fulling) given to the woven fabric, the range of style and mood is extended all the more.

Texture (the surface feel): The impression of the fabric's texture occurs in the feel and touch of its style and disposition, and also in the visual impression that it gives. In expressing the touch and feel of a fabric, detailed expressions are used. This is also an essential aspect of one's training, however, in actual design pictures one chooses those methods which will skillfully portray the visual impression. In short, design sketching where you draw many different pictures is different from illustrations whose details are drawn in with careful deliberation. One cannot afford to spend an awful lot of time in working on one picture. For this reason, it is important to touch and study the characteristics of the fabric and its quality beforehand, and to think out how to use the painting materials in order to give effective expression of the fabric. Further, it does not matter what kind of painting materials are used. Using a combination of different painting materials is also effective. In the manner of the design picture's finish, it is probably a good idea to draw the human figure, from a perspective of 3 meters away, which regards to garment shape, fabric sense, total body, face, and hair.

布地は使用される繊維の特徴（長い短い、太い細い）、捻りの強弱、配列、絡みの密度、又更に織られた布を後加工処理（起毛、縮じゅう）、などによって様々なタイプの風合いが作られています。

布のテクスチュアー（表面の質感）は風合いや肌合いなどの感触にある印象と、視覚的な印象とがあります。感触感を表現するには細密による表現が用いられ、これもトレーニングには欠かせませんが、実際のデザイン画では視覚的な印象を上手に演出する方を選びます。仕上り具合は丁度人物を３ｍ離れて見た印象で服の形、素材感全身、顔、髪、を描くと良いでしょう。つまり何枚も描くデザイン画は、じっくり描き込んだイラストレーションとはちがい、一枚の表現作業にあまり多くの時間を費やせないからです。そのため布地や材質の特徴を前もって観察し、画材の使い方を工夫し、簡略化し、効果的に表現することが大切です。また画材はどんなものを使ってもかまいません。

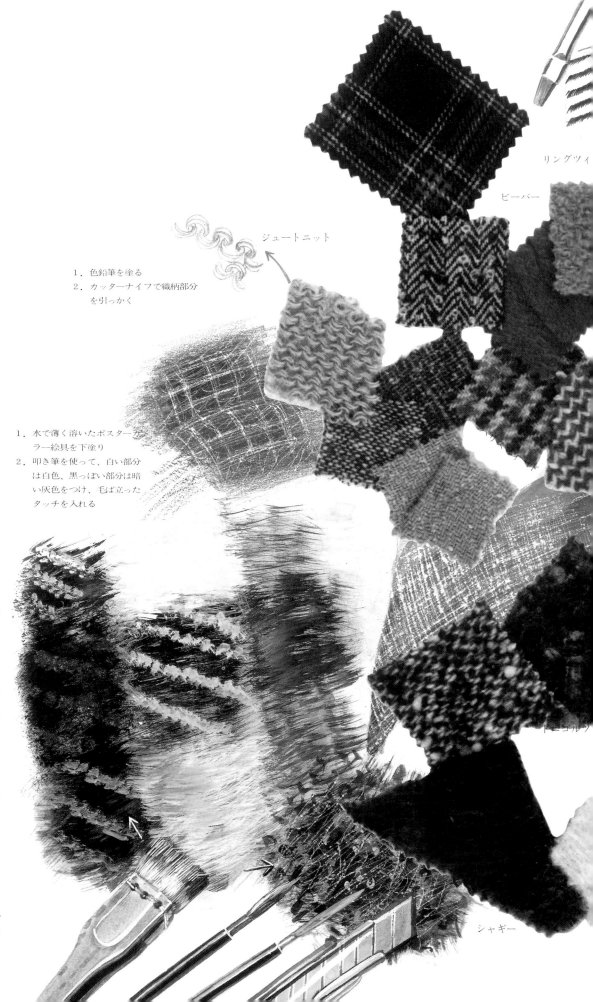

リングツイ

ビーバー

ジュートニット

1．色鉛筆を塗る
2．カッターナイフで織柄部分を引っかく

1．水で薄く溶いたポスターカラー絵具を下塗り
2．叩き筆を使って、白い部分は白色、黒っぽい部分は暗い灰色をつけ、毛ば立ったタッチを入れる

ドニゴルツ

シャギー

シェパードチェック

1. 水で薄く溶いたポスターカラー絵具を下塗り
2. 黒色のポスターカラー絵具を叩き筆につけ、紙で水気をとり、叩くようにタッチを入れる

グレンチェック

ドスキン

ハウンドツース

ヘアーライン

エナメルクロス

フラノ

チョークストライプ

バーズアイ

ペンシルストライプ

スウェード

グネップツィード　ネップ入れツィード

1. 水で薄く溶いたポスターカ　2. 白色のクレヨンエンピツで
　ラー絵具を下塗り　　　　　　ジグザグの織柄を入れる

3. 濃い目のポスターカラー絵具　4. カッターナイフで毛ば立っ
　を塗る　　　　　　　　　　　　たタッチを入れる

ツィル

ガンクラブチェック

ヘリンボーンツィード

35

PAINTING

●ウォーターカラーによる色出し

TIGHT-FIT LINE DRESS
タイトフィットラインドレス

透明水彩
着色部分に筆で水を含ませ、乾かないうちに用意した色で滲ませるように着色すると色が紙面に拡がっていきます。更に、濃く描きたい時は濃く溶いた絵具を最初の着色が乾かないうちに同様の方法で上から塗るようにします。この場合、ドライヤーを使うと色が固ってしまうことがあるので自然乾燥をさせ、乾いてからハイライトやアクセントカラーを加えるようにします。

6-
1- SKIN
2- HAIR
3- WATER
4-
5- HIGHLIGHT

Pastel White

WHITE

The left leg of the model is the pivot line, while the right leg stepping out creates the rhythm. Care should be taken with the slope of the shoulder, waist and knee lines.

モデルの右脚が支軸になって左脚の踏み出しにリズムをつくっています。肩、腰、膝線の傾斜に注意しましょう。

水彩、画用紙

Coloring is applied by using the concentration of the paint colors in an order of four steps.
The fourth color red is mixed with a little purple and is used for representing the shadowed portion of the costume.

着色は絵具の濃度を4段階で順に塗っていきます。4番目の赤は少し紫を混ぜコスチュームの陰の部分の表現に使います。

SHADOW

水彩、画用紙

FIT & TIERED LINE DRESS

フィット＆ティアードラインドレス

水彩、画用紙

ホワイトパステルで材
質の光りを入れ、指先
でこする。

Using a flat brush or a round brush,
the garment is painted with an equal
density overall, and by further painting repeated coats on those portions
that are dark or in shadow, the density is intensified.

平筆か丸筆を使って服全体を均等の
濃さで塗り、更に暗い、又は陰にな
っている部分を重ね塗りをし、濃さ
を深めます。

Portions which have special design
points or construction details are
drawn in with the light touch of a fine
brush, using the first coat color mixed
with a dark purple color.

デザインのポイント部分、構造上の
ディテールは地塗り色にダークな紫
を混ぜた色を使って細筆でタッチを
入れます。

TUBE LINE COAT
チューブラインコート

The flow of material, when it is plain and unpatterned, is difficult to capture, but can be clearly observed when the material has checks or stripes. By means of darts and patches, the change in the narrowed fabric pattern and the direction of the pattern on the collar and sleeves, can be captured and drawn well.

無地では把みにくい生地の流れが格子や縞でははっきりと観察できます。ダーツや切替えによる、身巾のゆるみやしぼり具合、衿、ラペル肩から袖へ流れる柄など、縞や格子の方向を正しく表現することが大切です。

Center

Shape

水彩、画用紙

RECTANGULAR LINE SUIT
レクタンギュラー (ストレート) ラインスーツ

Draw a rectangular silhouette and following on from that, draw in the characteristics of the shoulders, waist and skirt hemline, bringing the garment as a whole together. Special attention should always be paid to the line drawing which shows the body and the volume of the garment.

長方形のシルエットを描き、続いて肩、ウエスト、スカートの裾の特徴を描き加え全体をまとめます。
人体と服の分量感の関係がどのようになっているのか把む事が大切です。との部分でフィットし、又離れているのかよく観察してみましょう。

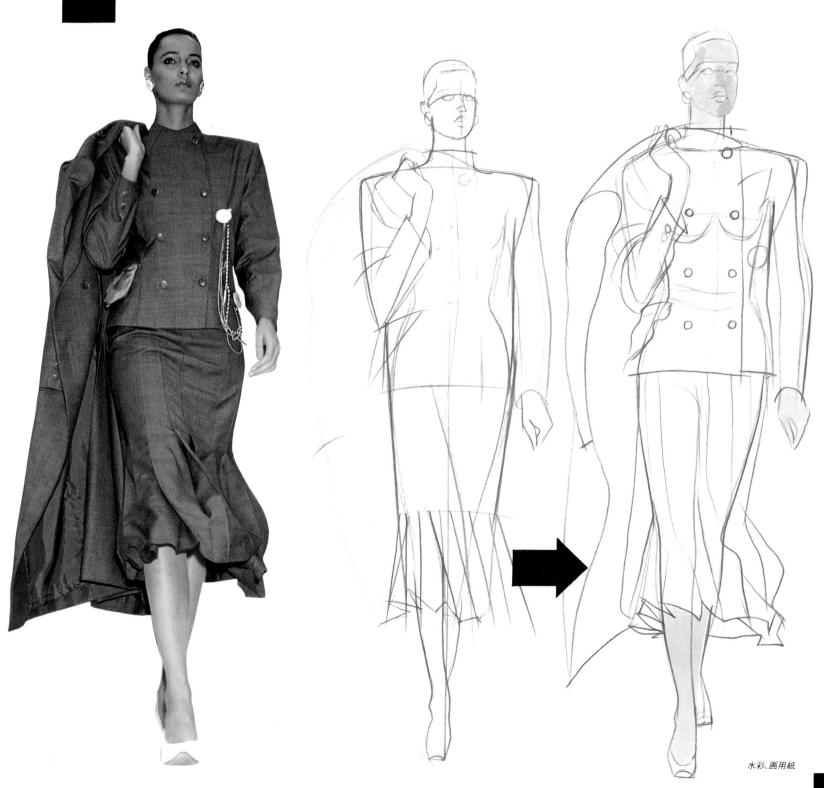

水彩、画用紙

43

MERMAID LINE DRESS

マーメイドラインドレス

A twisted pose is created by making the trunk the boundary for the movement between the upper half of the body and the lower half of the body.

上半身と下半身の向きが胴を境にして、ねじれたポーズになっています。

The costume is drawn following the line of the body (the legs).

コスチュームは体の線（脚部）に沿って描かれます。

●カラーペンシルによる色出し

By painting a light first coat in water color, then using a pencil over the top of this, the woven touch of the fabric's texture is expressed.

淡く水彩で地塗りをし、その上から
ペンシルを使って素材の織編タッチ
を表現します。

水彩、色鉛筆、ケント紙

JERSEY DRESS
ジャージイドレス

Knit materials which possess elasticity transmit the body's movement very minutely in the garment. The drape is drawn using soft curves.

For the first coat, water color is painted lightly all over the garment, and when it is dry touches are added for the fabric's texture in pastel color. Where pastels are painted in repeated layers on top of one another, spraying a fixative on the first painted surface, will give a more stable background color when painting the second coat, and it is possible to add tone to the depth of color.

In pastel paintings, one shouldn't be too concerned about fine details, rather the trick is to paint the picture boldly and dynamically.

伸縮性のある薄手のニット素材は体の動きを敏感に服に伝えます。

ドレープはソフトな曲線を使って描きます。

地塗りは水彩を淡く服全体に塗り、乾いてからパステルで材質のタッチ、を加えます。

パステルを重ねて塗る場合、一度塗った上から定着スプレーをかけ、再び塗ると地色が安定し、色の濃淡の調子をつけることができます。

パステル面では細部にこだわらず大きくダイナミックに描くことがポイントです。

WATER
COLOR
WHITE

pastel Pencil

PAST

水彩、パステル、ケント紙

TRAMPET LINE SUIT

トランペットラインスーツ

BLUE LIGHT

SIDE

SIDE

WATER

TINT

WATER

水彩、画用紙

· On the sleeves, body and skirt panels, avoiding the darts and seams, soak the surface of the paper in water and stain it with ink before it dries.
· Black is applied directly to those portions whose fabric surface is very small.
· The remaining unpainted portion is painted a bright color such as blue or yellow so as to represent light on the black color.
· Capture the extent of the body and the size of the garment.
· Poses which have movement, always have a soft line in the shape of the letter "S", which runs throughout the whole body from the top of the head to the tips of the toes.

・袖、身頃、スカートのパネルごとにダーツや縫い目を避けながら紙面に水を含ませ、乾かないうちに墨をおとしていく。
・素材面積の少ない部分は直接黒く塗る。
・塗り残しの部分はブルーやイエローのような明るい色を塗り黒色の光を表わす。
・体の分量と服の大きさをとらえる。
・動きのあるポーズはいつも頭の先からつま先にかけて全身にゆるいＳ字ラインが走る。

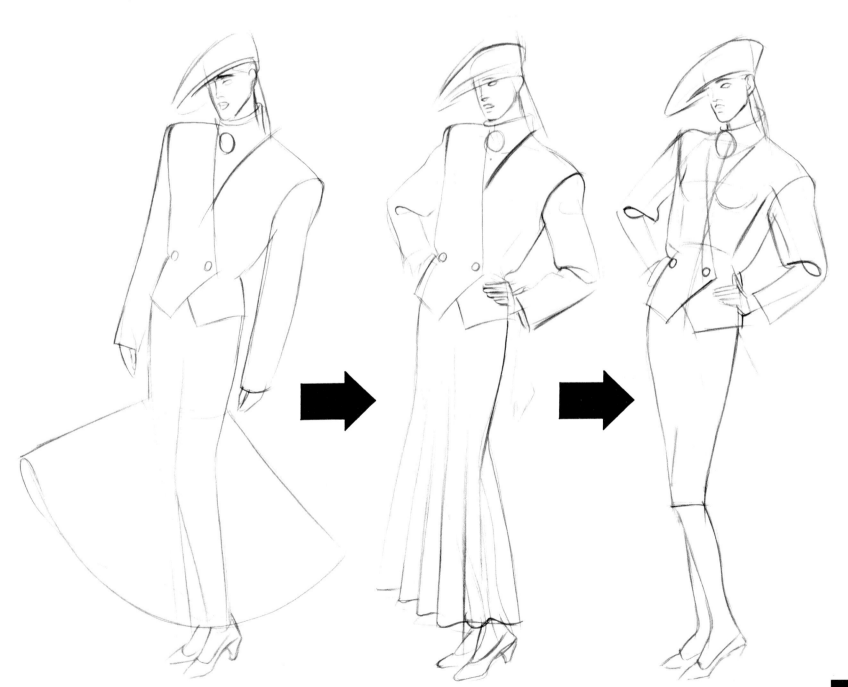

TAILORED

テーラード

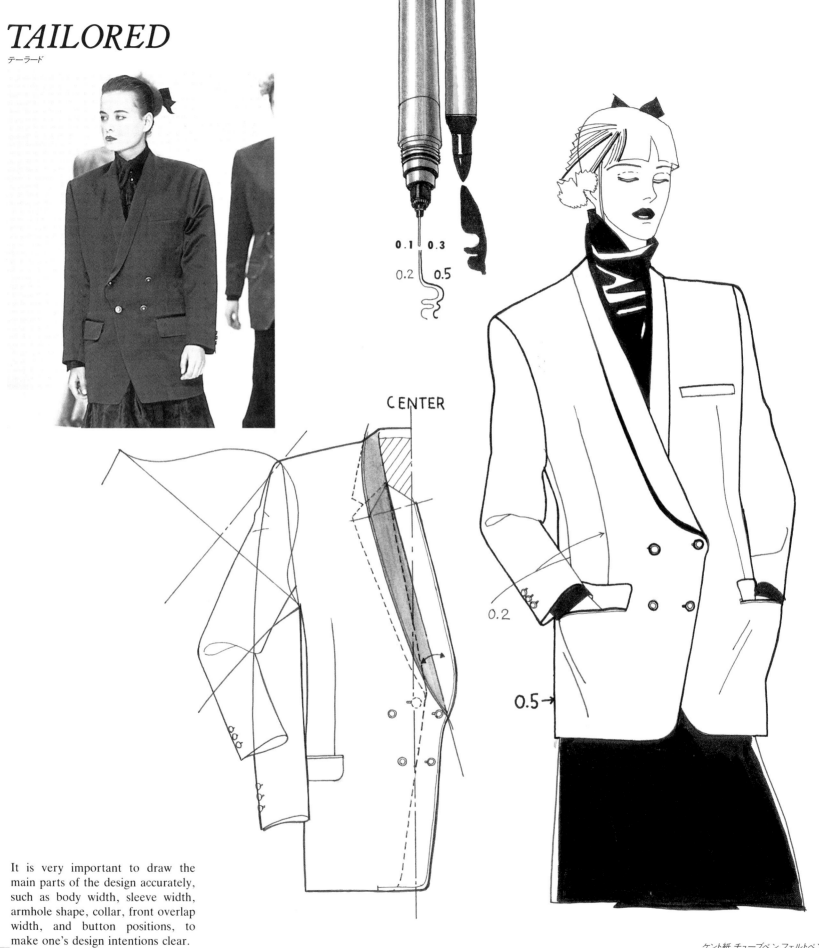

CENTER

0.1 0.3
0.2   0.5

0.2

0.5→

It is very important to draw the main parts of the design accurately, such as body width, sleeve width, armhole shape, collar, front overlap width, and button positions, to make one's design intentions clear.

ケント紙、チューブペン、フェルトペン

SHIRT JACKET
シャツジャケット

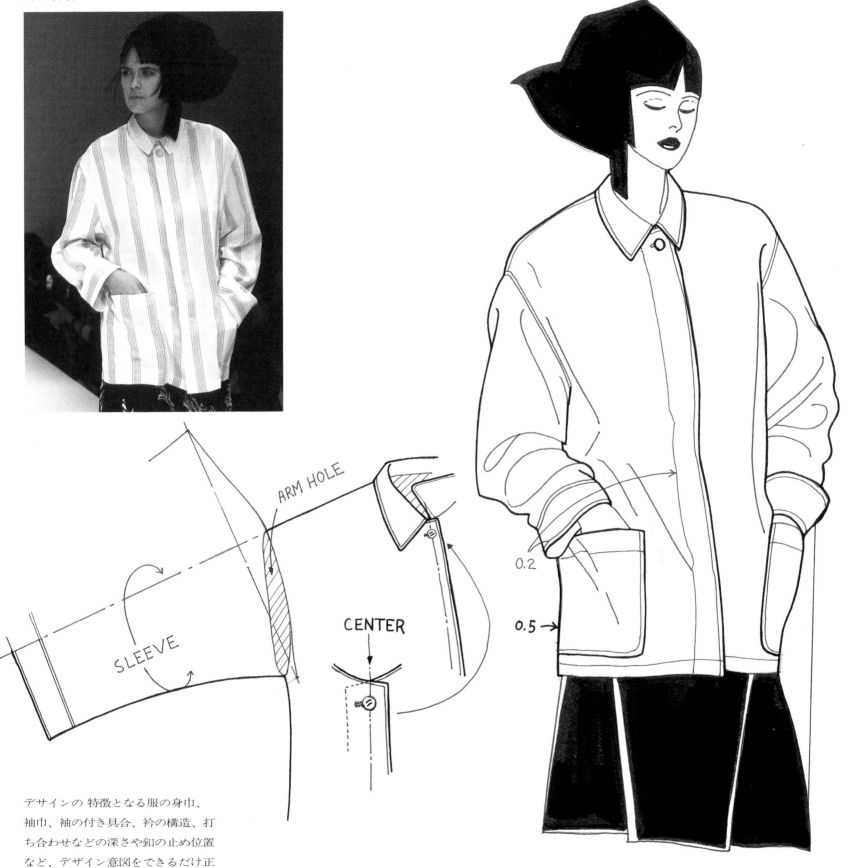

ARM HOLE

SLEEVE

CENTER

0.2

0.5

デザインの特徴となる服の身巾、
袖巾、袖の付き具合、衿の構造、打
ち合わせなどの深さや釦の止め位置
など、デザイン意図をできるだけ正
確に描くことが大切です。

ケント紙、チューブペン、フェルトペン

STRAIGHT LINE COAT
ストレートラインコート

1   2   3   4   5

濃淡の段差（エッジ）を
溶かし、なじませる。

画用紙、ポスターカラー

OFF-BODY LINE COAT

オフボディラインコート

鉛筆で大まかに形を描く

ほほやあご、鼻を白く残し、顔の地
塗りをする

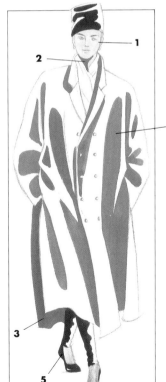

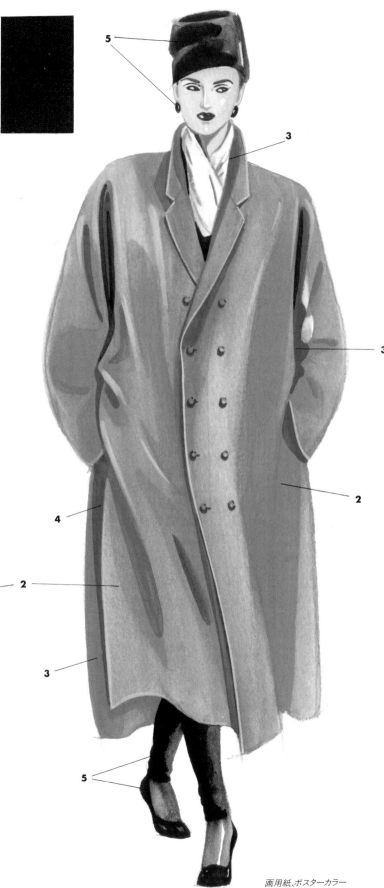

・モノトーンによる仕上げ

Prepare five shades of grey from light to dark on a pallet using poster colors. Paint the shadows in the drapes with dark grey first. Next wet a round brush with water, blur the edges of the different shades with the wet brush, and then finish the painting in a soft style.

ここではポスターカラーを使って5段階の明暗の灰色を、絵皿につくります。ドレープに出来る影の部分を地色の灰色で塗ります。次に水を適度に含ませた丸筆で、着色のエッジを溶かしなじませながら全体をソフトに仕上げます。

画用紙、ポスターカラー

BLOUSON
ブルゾン

When drawing models, we often emphasize certain parts of the body or clothing to set the mood of the clothing.
Here the leather blouson and skirt are drawn realisticly, and boldly, using conté.

服のイメージに重点を置き、ムード的に部分を強調して表現する場合があります。ここでは皮のブルゾンとスカートの力強いイメージをコンテを使ってリアルに描いています。

TENT LINE
テントライン

4 B、5 Bなどの濃い目の鉛筆を使ってスケッチを描き、定着液でスケッチを固定します。次に、短かく折ったパステルの腹の部分を紙面に当て、そのままこするようにタッチを入れます。

一度描いたタッチを定着液で固定し、乾いてから、再びタッチを入れると、濃度が強まります。

コンテ、ケント紙

DESIGN VARIATIONS

着装展開

By combining a variety of motifs with the initial design, you may discover interesting coordinates and styles, which will help you think of new design variations.
最初のデザイン画に関連したモチーフを組み合わせていくと、いろいろなコーディネイトのスタイルや着こなしが生まれ、それらがデザインバリエーショ

ンとなってイメージがふくらんでいきます。

SEE-THROUGH
シー・スルー

丸ペン、マーカー

不透明水彩
彩色に使う色はあらかじめ適量を絵
皿に溶かしておきます。ここでは帽
子、鳩の青、傘の青、ソックスのグ
リーン、スカートの濃い茶色、それ
に、ジャケット、ブラウス等々、一
着ごとに用意した色で塗り上げ、仕
上げはパステル、水彩のホワイトで
光沢のアクセントを入れます。

TEXTURE
ポスターカラーによる素材感

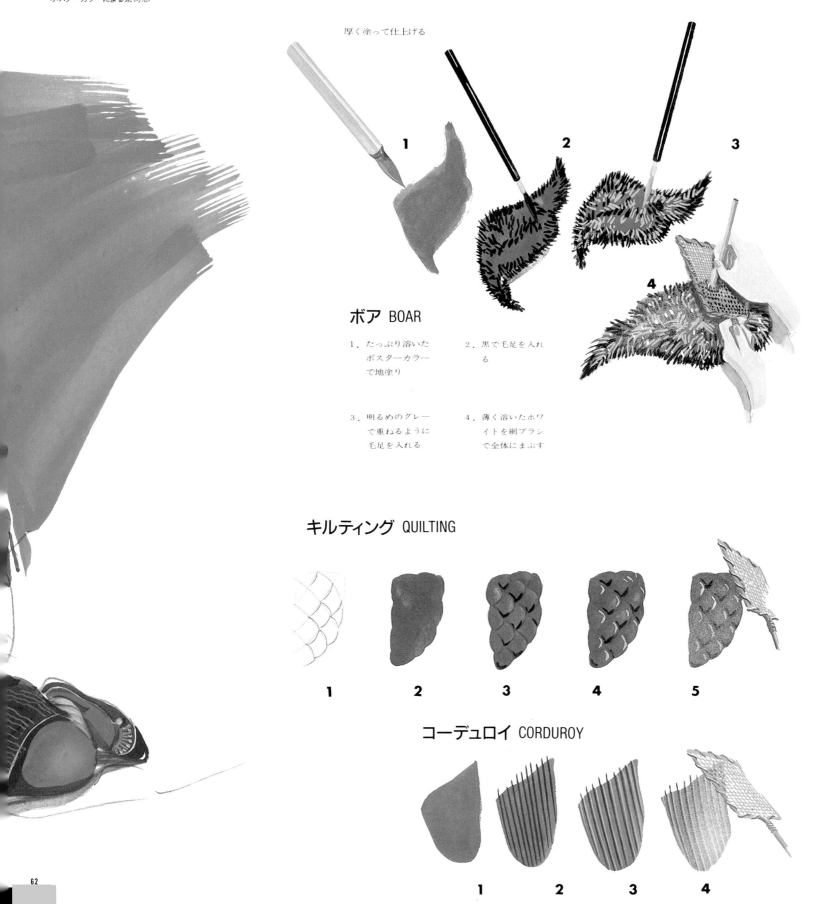

厚く塗って仕上げる

1　**2**　**3**

4

ボア BOAR

1. たっぷり溶いた
   ポスターカラー
   て地塗り

2. 黒で毛足を入れ
   る

3. 明るめのグレー
   で重ねるように
   毛足を入れる

4. 薄く溶いたホワ
   イトを網ブラシ
   で全体にまぶす

キルティング QUILTING

1　**2**　**3**　**4**　**5**

コーデュロイ CORDUROY

1　**2**　**3**　**4**

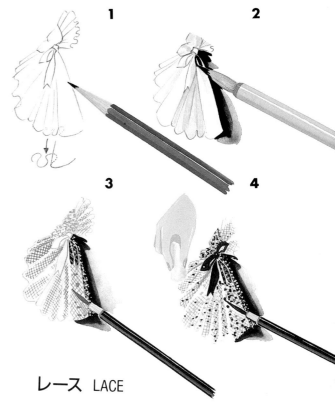

レース LACE

1. 布地の動きを確かめながら、奥から手前に型を描く

2. たっぷりと水を入れ、淡く溶いたグレーで影の部分を着色

3. 少し濃いめに溶いたグレーで、レースの網めをブロックごとに描く

4. 黒でタッチを入れ、ねり消しゴムで鉛筆の線を消す

プリント PRINT

ウーステッド WORSTED

1. たっぷりと溶いたポスターカラーで下塗り

2. 薄く溶いたグレー色で部分的にハイライト

3. 明るめのグレー色を面相筆で細く入れる

4. 網ブラシで薄く溶いたホワイトを散らす

SOFT COAT
ソフトコート

Felt pen ink penetrates paper very well. The color achieved depends on the absorbency of the paper used; the color will be very transparent and vivid on smooth paper, while it will be dark and subdued on rough watercolor paper.

フェルトペンのインクは浸透性に富み、描く紙の吸収性に対し、色の発色に違いが生じます。なめらかな紙面の上では透明度が高く、鮮明な色合いとなり、ざらつきのある水彩紙の上では、濃く、落ちついた色合いになります。

丈が長く、フイットしたスカートは
腰から脚にかけてスラリッとしたボ
トムのデザインにシルエットのポイ
ントがあります。デザイン画ではそ
うしたイメージをより一層印象づけ
る為、ポーズに工夫を凝らし、斜め
の動きをモデルにつけて表現してい
ます。

淡い色から先に塗り、色を重ねなが
ら次第に濃度をつけていきます。

FELT PEN

モデルをスケッチし、服のデザイン
とポーズの持ち味を組み合わせて着
装させます。

BIG LINE COAT
ビッグラインコート

コスチュームの素材感とボリュウム。　　コスチュームの形を分析する。

素描による人物とコスチュームとの　　タッチを描き加えた量感表現。　　ディフォルメによる拡大表現。
全体把握。

こするように絵具を伸ばしながら塗
り、乾き際に濃いオーカー色でシャ
ドーを塗り重ねていきます。

When we make design drawings, we sometimes use proportions different from standard model proportions. When modifying the standard proportions, the torso part of the bodys and clothing, that is, shoulders to waist to hips, should not be changed much. But emphasis is required on the arms and legs, while the head should be drawn slightly small.

私達はデザイン画を描く時、モデルのプロポーションを8頭身以外のバランスで描くことがあります。

基準となる8頭身のバランスを変えて描く場合、注意することは人体と服のトルソー部分（肩巾、ウエスト、ヒップラインまでの分量）をあまりくずさず描くことです。

強調する部分は腕、脚部が中心で、加えて頭部を一回り小さく描くようにします。

ポスターカラー、画用紙

GROUP

群像

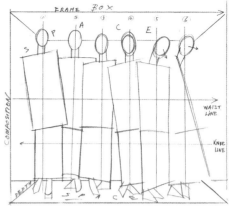

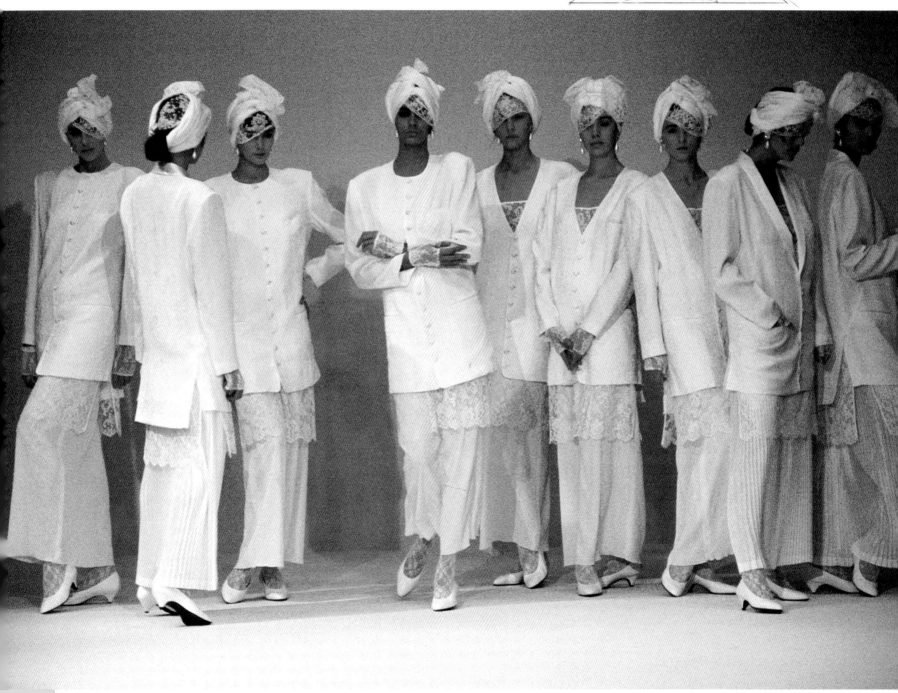

By means of the framework and dimension, a space which has walls and a floor and ceiling is created, and the positional lines of the knee and the body can be drawn. And then, when you layer the positioning of the garment (people) drawn with a generous line, it is possible to comprehend the position of people within the space.

枠と奥行きで壁面と天井、床を持つ空間をつくり、大体の位置に膝位置線と胴位置線を引きます。そして大まかなラインで描いた服（人物）を重ねて配置させると、空間の中の人物の位置がつかめてきます。

When you draw people with a black coating, their existence becomes all the more predominent. In this way, the group can be comprehended as one cluster and the sense of living movement can be evoked all the more definitely.

人物を黒塗りで描くと、いっそう存在感が現れてきます。このように群像を一つの固まりとして捉え、全体の動き存在感を一層確かなものにしていきます。

Next, we proceed by drawing in arms, body, legs and garment structure of the people in conjunction with their movements.

次に、固まりを一人一人の動きに合わせ腕や胴、脚、服の構造へと描き進めます。

上から見た場合の足跡の位置

ETHNIC
エスニック

セピア色のカラーインクを
使ってドレープの深さ浅さ
の明暗を重ね塗りで表現し
ます。

カラーインク,ケント紙

SKETCH

Sketchings of designs on various themes that have appeared in fashion magazines are very good materials for your designs and sketches.
First, select a full length figure from the articles, then cut it out from the background. When you do this, you will easily see the silhouette of the clothing, and depending on the deformatic technique in P 67, you can alter the balance of the size and length of the face, arms, and legs; then try to draw the silhouette in a similiar way in two dimensions. From here you go towards drawing the details of the clothing, and while doing countless sketchings, you can grasp the massiveness of the clothing. When you become able to draw with crisp line, you can finish them off by the colouring application method described in the preceeding section.

ファッション誌に載っている様々なテーマのデザインをスケッチしてみることはデザインやデザイン画を学ぶ大変良い練習になります。
まず全身の写真を選び、人物を背景から切り抜いてみます。そうすると服のシルエットが良くわかり、それをディフォルメの方法（P67）によって顔、腕、脚の大きさ、長さ、のバランスを変え、シルエットと同じように平面的に描いてみます。それから服の細部へと描き、何枚もスケッチするうちに服の量感がつかめてきます。線画でしっかり描けるようになったなら、前頁で解説している着彩方法をつかって仕上げてみましょう。

佐藤む美　鄭紗祇子(貞子)　　　　　　　　金子淮子　　　　　　　　金子祥江　　　　　　　　八木博史
EDITORIAL STAFF: / MUBI SATO　SADAKO TEI / ASSISTANT:　JUNKO KANEKO / MODELLISTE:　YOSHIE KANEKO　PHOTOGRAPHER: / HIROSHI YAGI

COOPERATION

KANSAI (KANSAI YAMAMOTO)
Tokyo central omotesando bldg. 515 4-3-15 Jingumae Shibuya-Ku Tokyo Japan

KENZO (KENZO TAKADA)
3 Place des Victoires 75001 Paris France

JUNKO KOSHINO
6-5-36 Minami Aoyama Minato-Ku Tokyo Japan

49AV JUNKO SHIMADA (JUNKO SHIMADA)
Kouchou Bldg. 2-1-6 Shibuya Shibuya-Ku Tokyo 150 Japan

NICOLE (ITSUKO NAKAJIMA)
Nicole Bldg 3-1-25 Jingumae Shibuya-Ku Tokyo 150 Japan

MADAME NICOLE (MITSUHIRO MATSUDA)
Nicole Bldg. 3-1-25 Jingumae Shibuya-Ku Tokyo Japan

INGEBORG   (ISAO KANEKO)
ANEX-B HILLSIDE TERRACE 2-30 Salugaku-Cho shibuya-Ku Tokyo Japan

YUKI TORII
5-7-16 Ginza Chuo-Ku Tokyo Japan

プロフィール
THE AUTHOR·ISAO YAJIMA

1945 長野県生れ
1945: Born in Nagano Prefecture, Japan
1966 桑沢デザイン研究所卒業
1966: Graduated from the Kuwazawa Design Institute of Tokyo
1966～1972 桑沢デザイン研究所在職
1966-1972: Instructor, Kuwazawa Design Institute of Tokyo
1972～1978 キャングループ企画顧問
1972-1978: Planning Consultant, CAN Group
1979～ ミラノに渡る
1979- : Milan, Italy
桑沢デザイン研究所ファッションドローイング 講師
Instructor of Drawing, Kuwazawa Design Institue of Tokyo
バンタンデザイン研究所 講師
Instructor, Vantan Design Institute
中国デザイン専門学校 講師
Instructor, Chugoku Design School
東京ファッションイラストスクール(通信教育講座)
Director, Correspondence Course, Tokyo Fashion Illustration School
現在、東京とミラノ(イタリヤ)にスタジオを持ち イラストレーション、デザインワークを行っている。
Isao Yajima is currently doing illustration and design work from his studios
in Tokyo and Milan, Paris.

エディトリアル： エディツオーニ ヘネッセン社(イタリヤ)との専属契約
MAJOR EDITORIALS: Edizione Hennessen S.R.L. (Italy)
イタリアンヴォーグ誌
Italian Vogue (Italy)
モンドウォモ誌
Mondouomo (Italy)
婦人画報社
Fujin Gaho (Japan)
文化出版局
Bunka Shuppan (Japan)
スタイル社
Style Sha (Japan)
etc.

専門誌及び広告： パルズィレーリ
PUBLICITY: Pal Zileri (Italia)
グルッポザネラ
Gruppo Zanella (Italia)
アイダブリュエス
IWS (Italia)
三菱レイヨン
Mitsubishi Rayon
テイジン
TEIJIN
織部企画
Oribe Planners
東京ルック(東京婦人子供服工業組合発行)
Tokyo Look
ワコール
WACOAL
キャングループ
CAN Group
コパン
Copan
アルジャン
Argent
インターナショナル ドウ プレタポルテ フェミニン アンド サロンブティック ポルト ド ベルサイユ パリ
INTERNATIONAL DU PRET A PORTER FEMININ & SALON BOUTIQUE PARIS PORTE DE VERSAILLES (FRANCE)
キティレコード
Kitty Record
三菱自動車
Mitsubishi Automobiles
etc.

著書： 東京ファッションイラストスクールテキスト(東京アカデミー出版)
PUBLICATIONS: Tokyo Fashion Illustration School Text
矢島功ファッションイラストレイテッド(織部出版)
Isao Yajima Fashion Illustrated
ファッションドローイング (グラフィック社)
Figure Drawing for Fashion(Graphic-sha)

モード ドローイング コスチューム(女性)
MODE DRAWING COSTUME(FEMALE)

1987年2月25日　第1刷発行
February 25, 1987 First Publication
1990年9月25日　第5刷発行
September 25, 1990 Fifth Publication
著者： 矢島　功(絵紗生)
Author: Isao Yajima
発行者： 久世　利郎
Publisher: Toshiro Kuze
発行所： 株式会社グラフィック社
Graphic-sha Publishing Company Limited
〒102東京都千代田区九段北1-9-12
1-9-12 Kudankita Chiyoda-Ku, Tokyo, Japan
Tel.03-263-4318 Fax.03-263-5297　振替・東京3-114345
企画・編集： アトリエKO
Planning, Layout, and Editing: ATORIE KO CO.,LTD.
東京都渋谷区神南1-5-14 三船マンション703
703 Mifune Mansion 1-5-14, Jinnan, Shibuya-Ku, Tokyo, Japan
Tel.03-464-8936 Fax.03-770-3465
印刷・製本： 日本写真印刷株式会社
Printing: *Nissha Printing Co., Ltd.*

ISBN4-7661-0391-2 C3071